DARE TO PROSPER

Catherine Ponder

DEVORSS *Publications*

Dare to Prosper
Copyright © 1983
by Catherine Ponder

ISBN: 0-87516-511-7
Library of Congress Catalog Number: 82-074520

Third Printing, 2000

DeVorss & Company, Publisher
P.O. Box 550
Marina del Rey, CA 90294

Printed in The United States of America

Other Books by Catherine Ponder

THE DYNAMIC LAWS OF PROSPERITY

THE DYNAMIC LAWS OF HEALING

THE PROSPERITY SECRET OF THE AGES

THE DYNAMIC LAWS OF PRAYER

THE HEALING SECRET OF THE AGES

OPEN YOUR MIND TO PROSPERITY

THE PROSPERING POWER OF LOVE

THE SECRET OF UNLIMITED PROSPERITY

OPEN YOUR MIND TO RECEIVE

THE PROSPERING POWER OF PRAYER

"The Millionaires of the Bible "Series

THE MILLIONAIRES OF GENESIS
Their Prosperity Secrets for You

THE MILLIONAIRE MOSES
His Prosperity Secrets for You

THE MILLIONAIRE JOSHUA
His Prosperity Secrets for You

THE MILLIONAIRE FROM NAZARETH
His Prosperity Secrets for You

CONTENTS

The *first* step to prosperous thinking: Creating a
vacuum to receive. Health is recovered after release of
grudge. Form a physical vacuum. Let go of unpleas-
ant relationships. The *second* step to prosperous
thinking: Getting definite about prosperity. Write
down your desires. Why settle for little when you can
have so much? Business expands through definite
thinking. The *third* step to prosperous thinking:
Mentally picturing your good. An alcoholic's healing
through imaging. The power of imagination. The
fourth step to prosperous thinking: Speaking daily affirmations. The power of spoken thoughts. Daily affirming brings couple their own business. Ancient
Hebrew prosperity affirmation still works. The *final*
step in prosperous thinking: Declaring prosperity
yours now! Be persistent.

INTRODUCTION:

YOU CAN JOIN THOSE WHO HAVE
DARED TO PROSPER

An Invitation From the Author

At a very low and lean period in my life, I was first introduced to the thought that I could and should "dare to prosper." That was several decades ago. I was fascinated with Charles Fillmore's prosperity teachings on this subject, and have used them with a gradually increasing success ever since. Although mine has not yet been a legendary "rags to riches" story, it certainly has been a "rags to enrichment story." And anyone can experience a similar "rags to enrichment story" who consistently uses the simple prosperity principles described in this book.

A friend, as a young girl, got to know Charles Fillmore personally while working at Unity Village, Missouri. One day she said to Mr. Fillmore, "I dreamed last night that I was 'so spiritual' that I could fly."

Charles Fillmore promptly replied, "That's fine, my dear. but are you also 'so spiritual' that you can pay the rent?"

That's what this book is all about!

THE PROSPEROUS RESULTS OF OTHERS

A reader in Kentucky wrote:

> I first began to read your ideas on prosperous thinking in 1963, and they have been my salvation. After my children finished college, left home and developed their own lives, I, too, enrolled in college. Through the use of prosperous thinking, I have now completed a B.A., a B.S., and a master's degree. I teach art, and am also working on another degree.
>
> In the midst of this heavy work and study schedule, I was faced with the challenge of my husband's untimely death. I love and bless you for

teaching me the basic truth: that God is the Source of my supply, as well as being my Comforter. These realizations have made possible so many new blessings.

To longtime readers, the material in this book may not seem new — only a reminder of universal principles of abundance that are available to all of us.[1] *These prosperity methods are recession-depression-and-inflation-proof, so that you will enjoy using them often!* Those readers who have most of my books may wish to pass this one on to others, as an introduction to prosperous thinking and its many benefits. A businessman in California recently said, "The practice of prosperous thinking has brought me back to God."

A longtime reader in Texas wrote:

Much that Dr. Ponder has written has been on healing: physical healing, healing of hard conditions, and healing of hard experiences. She has doctored the souls and spirits of those who have either studied with her personally over the years, or who have come to know her through her books, lectures and seminars. The divine ideas of abundance about which she writes

---

1. Much of the material found in this book first appeared in the Unity publications, and is used here by permission.

have been a healing balm and blessing to so
many people worldwide.

I trust that you, too, shall receive a healing
balm and a prosperity blessing as you now get
busy studying and applying the prosperity for-
mulas described herein, and also share them
with others. Together let us "dare to prosper!"

Catherine Ponder

P.O. Drawer 1278
Palm Desert, California, 92261
U.S.A.

DARE TO PROSPER

— Chapter 1 —

Prosperity comes not by chance but in accordance with absolute law. Charles Fillmore has said: "The law of supply is a divine law. This means that it is a law of mind and must work through mind." In other words, the peace, health, and plenty of prosperity must come through prosperous thinking. *The mind can be trained to think prosperously in simple, delightful ways, and the results of prosperous thinking are also delightful, practical, and satisfying.*

A businessman had had a serious heart condition most of his life. As he began to practice prosperous thinking, he relaxed more and more in mind, body, and affairs. As he began to

1

make his mind work for him in prosperous, healthy, victorious ways, tension disappeared; and after a time his physician stated that the heart condition had been healed. Today this man enjoys the best health of his life.

A lonely, unhappy career woman, who had often threatened suicide, learned about prosperous thinking, and became so fascinated with its practical power that she found new interests outside herself. She developed a new lease on life. The suicide talk stopped, and today she is a transformed individual.

A businessman who drank secretly found that as he began invoking prosperous thinking, he was able to resolve and dissolve inner hostilities and conflicts, through new, victorious attitudes. His desire to drink vanished.

In several instances, a marriage was saved after one of the partners learned of and began quietly to practice prosperous thinking. A widow who had been alone for twenty years remarried happily. One person's divorced partner returned, and they were remarried.

A businessman who had always detested his work discovered that as he applied prosperous thinking to his job, he got a whole new perspective on it. In due time, this man was sought out by many for counseling. Needless to say, he no longer considers his work detestable, and he enjoys the many contacts he has with others.

What were the simple but delightful steps these persons and many others took to invoke prosperous thinking, thus producing peace, health, and plenty in their lives?

THE FIRST STEP TO PROSPEROUS THINKING: CREATING A VACUUM TO RECEIVE

First, they got ready for the prosperity they desired by creating a vacuum to receive it. Nature abhors a vacuum and always rushes in with new substance to fill empty space, in mind, body, affairs, or relationships.

You, too, can form a mental vacuum by cleaning out of your mind negative, limited, unforgiving thoughts. As Charles Fillmore has written in his book, *Prosperity:*[1]

> Thoughts are things and occupy "space" in mind. We cannot have new or better ones in a place already crowded with old, weak, inefficient thoughts. A mental housecleaning is even more necessary than a material one.

If you are not sure what attitudes or memories need to be released and dissolved, give yourself a universal treatment in release and

1. Charles Fillmore, *Prosperity* (Unity Village, Mo; Unity Books, 1936).

forgiveness. Declare: "I FULLY AND FREELY FOR-
GIVE. I LOOSE AND LET GO. I CAST ALL JUDGMENTS,
RESENTMENTS, CRITICISM, AND UNFORGIVENESS
UPON THE CHRIST WITHIN, TO BE DISSOLVED AND
HEALED. THE PROSPERING TRUTH HAS SET ME
FREE TO MEET MY RICH GOOD AND TO SHARE MY
GOOD WITH OTHERS."

As you prayerfully affirm this, you will probably feel a sense of burden pass and a feeling of
release, relief, and freedom come. Your mental
vacuum for new good has now been formed.

HEALTH IS RECOVERED AFTER
RELEASE OF GRUDGE

A businessman became ill, and in spite of the
best medical care, he did not recover. His body
was filled with poison and nothing seemed to
dissolve it. One night while perspiring with a
high fever, this man realized that there must be
something he needed to get rid of or release
mentally or emotionally, since thoughts and
emotions have such a powerful effect on the
body. He then asked God to reveal what it was
that he needed to release.

Suddenly he began to think of a person
against whom he had been holding a strong
grudge and about whom he had said many un-

kind things. He then affirmed over and over: "I FULLY AND FREELY RELEASE AND FORGIVE. I LOOSE AND LET GO ALL ILL FEELING. DIVINE LOVE PRODUCES THE PERFECT RESULT NOW." Soon a feeling of peace, quietness, and release came, and he slept peacefully. The next morning his fever was gone and he recovered rapidly from his illness of many months' duration.

FORM A PHYSICAL VACUUM

Not only is it necessary to form a mental vacuum; often a physical vacuum must be formed. You can form a physical vacuum for new peace, health, and plenty by releasing, giving away, selling or otherwise getting rid of what you no longer want or need. Do not retain items of clothing, furniture, letters, files, books, or any other personal possessions that you no longer need or use. Get them out of the way to make room for what you do want. As long as you retain them, they take up space in your world that is needed for your new good. Declare to yourself as you go through your personal belongings: "I FULLY AND FREELY RELEASE. I LOOSE AND LET GO. I JOYOUSLY MAKE WAY FOR MY NEW GOOD, WHICH NOW APPEARS QUICKLY IN SATISFYING, APPROPRIATE FORM."

A widow had attempted in vain to settle her late husband's estate. Many legal entanglements had involved her with other heirs for almost a year. When she learned about forming a vacuum, she began cleaning out closets and other areas of her husband's clothes and personal possessions. The estate was quickly and harmoniously settled.

A widower, whose grief for his deceased wife had been intense for several years, found that as he freely and fully released her personal possessions his grief lessened and he was able to begin building a new life for himself.

A husband had asked his wife for a divorce and they were separated; then she learned of the vacuum law of prosperity. After she sold or otherwise disposed of a great many personal possessions left over from a former marriage, her present husband returned and they were happily reconciled.

LET GO OF UNPLEASANT RELATIONSHIPS

Sometimes it is necessary to form a vacuum by letting go of unsatisfying relationships and old ways of living that no longer please or satisfy. A woman who had had great financial needs found that new ideas and methods of work opened to her, after she gave up several dissatisfying friends of the past with whom she was no longer congenial. If there is a question in your mind about this possibility, affirm: "I NOW LET GO OLD WAYS OF LIVING, OLD, UNSATISFACTORY METHODS OF WORK, AND DISSATISFYING RELATIONSHIPS OF THE PAST. I AM NOW OPEN AND RECEPTIVE TO MY NEW AND HIGHEST GOOD."

THE SECOND STEP TO PROSPEROUS THINKING: GETTING DEFINITE ABOUT PROSPERITY

You are now ready to take the second step in prosperous thinking. Charles Fillmore described this step when he wrote:[2]

Go into the silence daily at a stated time and concentrate on the substance of Spirit prepared for you from the foundation of the world. This opens up a current of thought that will bring prosperity into your affairs.

Daily become still, and think about rich, unlimited substance of the universe that is everywhere present for you to form as prosperous ideas, which will produce prosperous results.

---

2. Ibid.

Affirm: "THE RICH SUBSTANCE OF THE UNIVERSE INSTANTLY RESPONDS TO MY PROSPEROUS THINKING. I AM NOW RICH IN MIND AND MANIFESTATION."

WRITE DOWN YOUR DESIRES

At this point begin definitely to mold substance. Do this by sitting quietly every day and writing down on paper what you feel you want to be, have, accomplish, and experience for the day, week, month, or year.

Dare to be definite about prosperity, if you want prosperity to be definite in manifesting for you. People often hesitate to write down and think about what they really desire. They do not realize that the mind is the connecting link between man and the rich but unformed substance of the universe. If you never think definitely about the prosperous results you desire, no mental contact is made with the rich substance of the universe; you must drift along in a stream of limitation and dissatisfaction.

A businesswoman attended a lecture on prosperous thinking and learned of the power of writing down her desires. She hurried home and made a list of the prosperous results she strongly desired in her life. Four days later a large sum of money, to which she had long been legally entitled but had been unable to collect, came to her.

WHY SETTLE FOR LITTLE WHEN
YOU CAN HAVE SO MUCH?

The rich substance of the universe is yours to do with as you wish. Why settle for so little in life when you can have so much, just by daring to be definite in your thinking? Another businesswoman, a widow, began writing out her true desires daily, at the first of a new year. She wrote down her desire to remarry happily. She wrote down her desire for a better home. She also stipulated her deep desire for a better paying, more satisfying job. In the middle of the year, a pleasant, better paying position was offered to her. At about the same time, she met her future husband, through mutual friends. They were married by the end of the year. He was a building contractor, and he gave her the better home she wanted. As he, too, began deliberately to practice prosperous thinking, he developed two other successful businesses.

When you write down your desires for the day, week, or month, list what you really want —not what you think you should have, nor what somebody else thinks you should have. Your deep-seated desires are God's good tapping at the door of your mind. Furthermore, write down dates by which you wish your desired good to be accomplished. You will be amazed at how the substance of heaven and earth will hasten to do your bidding when you give it definite desires and dates through which to work out good results.

BUSINESS EXPANDS THROUGH
DEFINITE THINKING

A businessman had long desired larger and better business property, for the expansion of his business. After learning of the power of prosperous thinking, he no longer hesitated to believe he could have the property; instead, he wrote down his definite desires for it. Soon he learned of a desirable piece of business property, and upon investigation found that it was priced quite reasonably. Everyone involved— his lawyer, the realtor, and the seller—tried to assist him in every way. Even the local bank president seemed interested in helping him acquire the property. It was as though all the forces of heaven and earth willingly co-operated to work out the financial arrangements, and this man soon settled his business in the new location.

As you get your desires down on paper, feel free to work and rework them, changing, revising, expanding, and rearranging them as you wish from day to day. Make lists of what you do not want in your life, and write down, concerning them, "BE THOU DISSOLVED, IN THE NAME OF JESUS CHRIST." Make lists of what you do want and write down, "THIS OR SOMETHING BETTER, FATHER. LET THY HIGHEST GOOD NOW MANIFEST. LET THE DIVINE RESULT NOW APPEAR." By decreeing the divine result, you remain open and receptive to your highest good, which may appear in the form of greater good than you had humanly conceived in your own private desires.

THE THIRD STEP TO PROSPEROUS THINKING: MENTALLY PICTURING YOUR GOOD

You are now ready to take the third step in prosperous thinking. Begin, at this point, to image your desires as already fulfilled. Mentally live with the picture of fulfillment as you go about your day. Do not try to reason through your mental pictures of fullfillment, or to understand how they are to come about. Just dare to image the fulfilled result as best you can, and then let the rich substance of the universe produce that imaged good in either usual or unusual ways. For your mental images declare often: "THIS OR SOMETHING BETTER, FATHER. LET THY HIGHEST GOOD NOW MANIFEST. LET THE DIVINE RESULT NOW APPEAR IN THE DIVINE WAY."

AN ALCOHOLIC'S HEALING
THROUGH IMAGING

A businessman's wife seemed to be a hopeless alcoholic. She was high-tempered, irresponsible, and very difficult to live with. She and her husband were on the brink of divorce when he learned that mental images make the conditions of mind, body, affairs, and relationships. He persistently began imaging his wife as peaceful, harmonious, responsible, easy to live with, and healed of alcoholism. For months he daily dared to image her as whole in mind, body, affairs, and relationships. Gradually she became calmer, more peaceful and harmonious. She then began taking more interest in herself, her husband, and life generally. I recently had lunch with this couple, and it was apparent that they are healthier, happier, and more prosperous than ever before. Furthermore, this woman's healing and resulting transformation are now complete.

THE POWER OF IMAGINATION

Psychologists declare that imagination is one of the mind's strongest powers. The more you dare to image your desired good as a fulfilled result, and the more you dare to live your mental images, the faster the imaging power of the mind will begin producing almost magical results for you. Your mental images make your conditions, but it is up to you to make your mental images of the good you desire. You should image only the highest and best you can conceive, because, "Whatever you image yourself as doing, you can do." (The wheel of fortune method is powerful, delightful, and helpful in developing the imaging power of the mind to produce prosperous results.)[3]

THE FOURTH STEP TO PROSPEROUS THINKING: SPEAKING DAILY AFFIRMATIONS

The fourth step in prosperous thinking is to begin affirming verbally, definitely, and daily

3. See Chapter 7 of *The Millionaires of Genesis* by Catherine Ponder for instructions on how to make a wheel of fortune. (Published 1976 by DeVorss & Co., Marina del Rey, California, 90291).

the divine manifestation of your desires. As you daily write down your desires and image them as fulfilled, affirm: "MY WORLD IS THE PERFECT CREATION OF DIVINE SUBSTANCE. THE FINISHED RESULTS OF DIVINE SUBSTANCE NOW APPEAR AS PEACE, HEALTH, AND PLENTY IN MY WORLD." In the beginning the world was created by definite, spoken affirmations, as God declared, "Let there be. . ." You can and should create your world accordingly, because you are created in the image and likeness of God, and you, too, have the power to form substance through your definite, spoken decrees for good.

An interior decorator had been out of work for several months and was $2,500 in debt. During a summer slack season she heard about the power of prosperous thinking in overcoming financial lack. She began imaging $2,500 in her checking account to pay all debts, and daily affirmed that her world was the perfect creation of divine substance; that the finished results of divine substance were appearing as peace, health, and plenty in her world. Almost immediately, a friend of a former customer telephoned and asked her to consider decorating an entire apartment house. Her estimate, running into thousands of dollars, was accepted; she was given the decorating job, and her commission amounted to $2,500. This proved to be only the first of a number of profitable jobs that have come to her. She is still joyously affirming: "MY WORLD IS THE PERFECT CREATION OF DIVINE SUBSTANCE. THE FINISHED RESULTS OF DIVINE SUBSTANCE NOW APPEAR AS PEACE, HEALTH, AND PLENTY IN MY WORLD."

THE POWER OF SPOKEN THOUGHTS

It is good to be systematic in the daily, verbal use of affirmations, by speaking them aloud in privacy for at least five minutes at a time, three times a day. There is increased power in spoken words to produce definite, satisfying, immediate results. Thinking the right thought is powerful, but speaking it forth into the rich substance of the universe in deliberate, definite, verbal form, over and over daily, gathers that rich substance together in definite events and circumstances that produce immediate, satisfying, and definite results. Charles Fillmore has explained:

Substance is first given form in the mind. . . . In laying hold of substance in the mind and bringing it up into manifestation we play a most important part. We do it according to our decree.[4]

---

4. Fillmore, *Prosperity*.

A little positive assertion and declaration of the good you desire is often all that is needed to turn the tide of events that will produce that good for you, swiftly and easily. How often have you talked about what you did *not* want, and gotten it? Now dare to speak of what you desire, and begin receiving it. The promise is: "Thou shalt also decree a thing, and it shall be established unto thee." (Job 22:28)

DAILY AFFIRMING BRINGS COUPLE THEIR OWN BUSINESS

A man and his wife were salaried employees, barely making a living. They learned about affirmations, and began daily affirming a better income. Soon the man, a draftsman, got the idea of designing greeting cards. His greeting cards soon became so popular that he and his wife left their jobs and went into the greeting-card business full time. Their income has greatly increased, and their greeting cards have become widely known and purchased.

ANCIENT HEBREW PROSPERITY AFFIRMATION STILL WORKS

Use definite affirmations for prosperity when you want definite prosperity results. For the purpose of prosperity the ancient Hebrews affirmed "Jehovah-jireh" when they wished to concentrate on substance. This means " 'Jehovah will provide,' the mighty One whose presence and power provides, regardless of any opposing circumstance."

A woman who owned some rental apartments began affirming, "JEHOVAH-JIREH, THE LORD NOW RICHLY PROVIDES," during a summer off-season period. Almost immediately her realtor rented one of the apartments for the next season, for $1,900. In another instance, a couple were in financial straits when they learned of the ancient Hebrews' prosperity affirmation. As they affirmed, "JEHOVAH-JIREH, THE LORD NOW RICHLY PROVIDES," the way opened for them to sell for cash some property that they had previously felt they might have to mortgage heavily. Another couple's mortgage payments were overdue and they feared losing their home; then they learned of the Hebrews' prosperity affirmation and began affirming, "JEHOVAH-JIREH, THE LORD NOW RICHLY PROVIDES." Neither had been able to find work for several months. Within a few days the husband obtained work and his wife was offered not one but two jobs, both of which offered higher salaries than any she had previously received. They did not lose their home, and began paying off many miscellaneous debts as well.

THE FINAL STEP IN PROSPEROUS THINKING: DECLARING PROSPERITY YOURS NOW!

After beginning to get rid of what you do not want by forming a vacuum; after writing out your desires, imaging and affirming their divine fullfillment, you are ready for the culminating step in prosperous thinking. The time has come to go about your daily activities, acting as though you are already prosperous, doing whatever you can to make it so in your times of work, play, and rest. This you are to do, however, in a very special way: by invoking the thought of success and prosperity with everything you think, say and do.

Deliberately become a prosperous thinker by beginning to think of yourself and others as successful, prosperous, victorious. Think often of whatever success, prosperity, and victorious good you are already enjoying, and give thanks for it. Declare to yourself often: "EVERY DAY IN EVERY WAY I AM GROWING MORE PROSPEROUS, SUCCESSFUL, VICTORIOUS. I AM MADE FOR PEACE, HEALTH, AND PLENTY, AND I AM NOW EXPERIENCING THEM IN EVER-INCREASING DEGREES IN MY LIFE." Give others the same thought whenever you think of them.

This is a delightful mental process to which your mind will quickly respond. Stop thinking of the failures and mistakes of yourself or others, and start concentrating on every degree of prosperity, success, and good that has been or is now evident. The mind is strengthened and uplifted by, and thrives on thoughts, images, and words of success; whereas it seems to shrivel and be repelled by thoughts, images and words of failure, limitation, and poverty. The mind delights in helping a prosperous thinker become more prosperous. That is why "nothing succeeds like success." Invoke the law of increased success by affirming: "MY SUCCESS IS BIG, POWERFUL, AND IRRESISTIBLE. NOTHING SUCCEEDS LIKE SUCCESS. I NOW GO FROM SUCCESS TO GREATER SUCCESS, IN THE NAME OF JESUS CHRIST."

Speak in terms of your good rather than in terms of apparent problems. Speak in terms of your blessings rather than in terms of your challenges. Emphasize the good in your life, knowing that as you do, it will increase. How often have you used the law of decrease and talked problems, difficulties, failure, limitation, ill health, confusion, inharmony? Now let your every act, tone, look, word express a quiet, confident assurance of success. Also, give yourself the thought of increased good by thinking of yourself as already looking, acting, and living as successfully and prosperously as you truly desire to be. Think of yourself as already wearing the clothes you wish to wear; as already living in a gracious, abundant manner; as already experiencing the health, prosperity, and happines you so rightly desire. Then speak positively, appreciatively, of every degree of health, prosperity, and happiness you are already experiencing. This will help to multiply your good.

BE PERSISTENT

There is just one other thing to remember: You must persist in doing these simple and delightful things step by step, day by day. Perhaps your mind has been steeped in thoughts, images, and words of failure, limitation, problems, and difficulties. If so, it may take a little while to clear your mind of the negative and make way for positive results. It is important that you persevere.

A successful writer once said something that has helped me persist past discouragement to success many times:

Before success comes in any man's life, he is sure to meet with much temporary defeat and, perhaps, some failure. When defeat overtakes a man, the easiest and most logical thing to do is to QUIT. That is exactly what the majority of men do.

More than five hundred of the most successful men this country has ever known told the author their greatest success came just one step *beyond* the point at which defeat had overtaken them.

So, if discouragement besets you and your deep longings seem in vain, just hang on to the thought: "NOTHING IN THE WORLD CAN TAKE THE PLACE OF PERSISTENCE AND DETERMINATION. WITH GOD'S HELP I NOW PERSIST INTO MY HIGHEST GOOD." Persevere in this idea.

Truly, the peace, health, and plenty of prosperity come not by chance but in accordance with the laws of prosperous thinking. *You* can invoke prosperous thinking for simple, practical, delightful results, as so many others have done.

SUBSTANCE—THE KEY TO PROSPERITY

— Chapter 2 —

A lady vacationed in Europe at the height of the depression in the 1930's. When a friend inquired how she could do such a thing, she mystically replied, "DIVINE SUBSTANCE IS THE ONE AND ONLY REALITY. THEREFORE, I HAVE PLENTY OF EVERYTHING NOW!" The friend who heard this explanation began to study the subject of substance as the key to prosperity. She became a prosperous housewife, and later a prosperity teacher to others.

A reader of mine recently wrote: "I don't believe in recessions! I watched my mother

22

become rich during the depression of the 1930's when she dwelled upon 'the rich substance of the universe' instead of dwelling upon appearances of financial limitation."

So instead of fretting about recession, depression, inflation or the high cost of living, dwell on "divine substance." When you dare to declare daily that "DIVINE SUBSTANCE IS THE ONE AND ONLY REALITY" in your life and affairs, you are well on the way to solving your own ills as well as helping to solve the ills of mankind. As a friend in Texas has said: "My greatest prosperity demonstrations have always come from using 'divine substance' affirmations."

THE NATURE OF SUBSTANCE

What is substance? The dictionary describes it as "that which underlies all outward manifestations; real, unchanging essence or nature of a thing." Jesus might have been referring to omnipresent substance when He spoke of the kingdom of heaven being at hand. Metaphysicians have described substance as "mind essence" or "thought stuff."

Charles Fillmore said:[1]

---

1. Fillmore, *Prosperity*.

This inexhaustible mind substance is available
at all times and in all places to those who have
learned to lay hold of it in consciousness. . . .
The spiritual substance from which comes all
visible wealth is never depleted. It is right with
you all the time and responds to your faith in it
and your demands upon it.

We are always molding inexhaustible mind
substance through our mental concepts,
whether we are aware of it or not. But often we
mold tangible things, conditions, and experiences that we do not want, by holding concepts
of disease, inharmony, old age, and financial
lack.

We can consciously and deliberately take control of our world by taking control of our attitudes about substance. The truth about substance is that it is mind essence which is present
in all, through all, and around all. But this in-
destructible, inexhaustible substance is handled
by the thoughts of the mind, which make it use-
ful as visible results.

We should constantly think of and appreciate
substance, because substance contains every element of good: life, love, wisdom, power, all
good. But since substance is passive, it waits
upon man to form it as he will; it comes forth in

man's world according to his thoughts and
words of good or of limitation. The world was
created in the beginning out of substance when
Jehovah God said, "Let there be." We create
our world out of substance in like manner.

If there seems to be dissatisfaction in any
phase of your life, affirm: "DIVINE SUBSTANCE IS
THE ONE AND ONLY REALITY IN MY LIFE, AND I AM
NOW SATISFIED WITH DIVINE SUBSTANCE." For more
definite needs declare: "DIVINE SUBSTANCE AP-
PROPRIATELY MANIFESTS FOR ME HERE AND NOW."

Still other powerful affimations to help you
mold substance as prosperous results are these:
"DIVINE SUBSTANCE CANNOT BE DIMINISHED. DI-
VINE SUBSTANCE CANNOT BE EXHAUSTED. DIVINE
SUBSTANCE CANNOT BE WITHHELD. DIVINE SUB-
STANCE CANNOT BE TAKEN. DIVINE SUBSTANCE IS
EVERYWHERE PRESENT, AND I WISELY USE IT NOW.
DIVINE SUBSTANCE IS THE ONE AND ONLY REALITY
AND DIVINE SUBSTANCE NEVER FAILS TO MANIFEST.
THE FINISHED RESULTS OF DIVINE SUBSTANCE NOW
APPEAR IN RICH APPROPRIATE FORM."

FINANCIAL GAINS IN BUSINESS

A businessman whose stock market transactions had been unsuccessful during the previous

year found that, as he began to declare substance as the only reality in his financial affairs, his success began to manifest. Within two months, his profits were greater than in the previous twelve months.

The owner of a cleaning plant watched his business increase weekly after he began affirming substance as the only reality in his financial affairs (even though three other cleaning plants in the same area closed down during this period). In fact, this man's volume increased $400 a week over that of the preceding month, after he began thinking of substance as the key to his prosperity.

A housewife who received an annual income from a relative's estate did not receive her check at the usual time. After affirming divine substance as the one and only reality in her financial affairs, the check finally arrived — late, but three times as large as the previous year's check.

Another housewife was affirming divine substance as the one and only reality in the financial affairs of her husband, when he was offered the best engineering job he had ever had. Furthermore, his new employer insisted that his starting salary be $100 more per month than he was asking!

DOCTOR EXPANDS HIS PRACTICE

Physical science has discovered that everything can be reduced to a few primal elements, and that if the universe were destroyed it could be built up again from a single cell. In like manner *we can expand or rebuild our financial world from a single right attitude about substance.*

A doctor proved the expanding power of right attitudes about substance. As he began to affirm that divine substance was the one and only reality in his financial affairs, an insurance company employed him to treat its company salesmen, his fees to be paid promptly by the company itself. This assignment was in addition to his already successful private practice.

As he continued to affirm substance as the one and only reality in his financial affairs, another interesting prosperity result appeared: Two years previously he had attempted to purchase a piece of business property, but the owner asked twice the amount the doctor felt led to pay. So the doctor dismissed the matter from his mind, thinking that if the property was his by divine right, he would be able to purchase it at the price he felt was right.

After he began affirming substance as the only reality, the owner of the property came to

him and stated that he now wished to sell the
business property. Having no other buyers,he
was ready to sell it at the original price, which
was half the amount he had been asking for the
last two years — and exactly what the doctor had
felt led to pay!

DAILY MEDITATION MAKES A MILLIONAIRE

Charles Fillmore has given some good advice
on how to realize substance as the key to your
prosperity:[2]

Daily concentration of mind on Spirit and its
attributes will reveal that the elemental forces
that make all material things are here in the
ether awaiting our recognition and appropria-
tion. It is not necessary to know all the details of
the scientific law in order to demonstrate prosperity. Go into the silence daily at a stated time
and concentrate on the substance of Spirit prepared for you from the foundation of the
world. This opens up a current of thought that
will bring prosperity into your affairs.

I recently read a news report about a young
man who, though not yet thirty, has become

_____

2. Ibid.

vice-president of an insurance company. For several years he has made it a habit to concentrate daily on substance. This man realized several years ago the power of his thoughts and words for success or failure, and he began spending an hour every morning thinking about substance and molding it in definite detail with his thoughts. During this morning hour, he mentally planned his day as he wished it to be, and he held in mind the figures of sales he wished to obtain.

Later, when he was placed in charge of a group of insurance salesmen, he spent time each morning thinking of them and the amount of sales he wished them to make that day. It was by this daily, faithful process of molding substance as he wished it to be, for himself and for others, that he worked his way up to the vice-presidency of his company. It has been predicted that he will be a millionaire by the time he is thirty-five.

MEDITATION BRINGS GIFTS OF GROCERIES

A housewife has described how daily meditation upon substance filled her grocery shelf. Prior to spending this time daily, she never had enough groceries on hand to feed the relatives and friends who often visited in her home. Then, as she began to meditate daily upon substance as the one and only reality, everyone who came to visit began bringing gifts of groceries and food. One relative began bringing fresh seafood from the coast where he lives. Another brought fresh bread, cakes, and pies from the bakery where he works. This woman says that now her freezer and pantry shelves are constantly filled with groceries.

SUBSTANCE OBEYS YOUR THOUGHTS

With every silent thought, as well as with every spoken word, you are telling substance what to do, and it obediently carries out whatever beliefs you hold in mind about it. In your silent thoughts as well as in your spoken words, give your attention to the richness of substance. It will seem as though heaven and earth are working together to produce satisfying results for you.

One Truth student says that her money goes much further when she shops, if she is "dressed up." By wearing her best clothes, even when she shops at the corner grocery store, she has a feeling of being prosperous. Others who come in contact with her unconsciously think of her as prosperous, and give her the benefit of their attitudes. The result is that her money seems to go further, and she seems able to buy more. It is as though substance is pleased, and multiplies for her.

When you give substance your appreciative attention, it seems to work overtime in many ways to meet your needs. A salesman who heard a lecture on substance went out the next day and immediately made a $1,200 sale to a customer who had previously given him only very small orders.

By declaring substance to be the one and only reality, you can cause old, dissatisfying conditions to fade away. By declaring the satisfying reality of substance, you can cause your mind to be filled and strengthened with new ideas, and your body to be renewed with vitality, energy, and renewed health. By declaring substance as the only reality, you place yourself in a position to witness the riches of the universe as they flow to you on every hand, in whatever form is most appropriate at the moment.

LOST FRIENDSHIP RENEWED

A merchant once had a customer whose friendship he apparently had lost. The former business friend had been writing him unfriendly letters. Instead of retaliating, the merchant sat down and mentally reworked the situation as he wished it to be, seeing the customer as friendly and co-operative, rather than as he appeared at the moment.

The merchant also affirmed that divine substance was the one and only reality in the situation, and that divine substance would not fail to make the situation right for all concerned. When he was able after several quiet periods to get a genuine feeling of friendliness, kindness, and good will toward the other man, he wrote him a letter just the opposite of those received: words of kindness, stating the merchant's desire that their friendship and business association might continue. He wrote, "My wish for you and your business is happiness, prosperity, and abundant good, and my continued thought for you shall be for your prosperity."

It was not long before the other man's attitude had changed completely, and the two men found themselves in complete harmony again. In fact, the merchant sold his friend $5,000 worth of merchandise shortly after this!

Conscious union between substance and man is made within the mind of man. Knowing this, you no longer need feel that something or some-

body can keep your financial supply from you. Indeed, you begin to realize that through your right understanding of substance, all things can be accomplished within the mind first.

THE AUTHOR'S EXPERIENCES WITH
DIVINE SUBSTANCE

In my own experience, I have proved to my complete satisfaction the power that is generated by giving substance my conscious thought. In one instance, while I sat in my study completing some writing assignments that were due, I suddenly realized how hungry I was; but there seemed to be no time to go out and eat. So I affirmed: "DIVINE SUBSTANCE IS THE ONE AND ONLY REALITY AND DIVINE SUBSTANCE NEVER FAILS. THE FINISHED RESULTS OF DIVINE SUBSTANCE NOW APPEAR IN THIS SITUATION IN APPROPRIATE FORM."

Within a few minutes I received a telephone call from a neighbor, whom I had never met. She had seen the light on in my study and realized I was working late. She wondered if I would consider sharing a meal she had already cooked; she said that if I would, she would send it over to me on a tray, while it was still warm. Within a few minutes from the time I had made my affirmation, I was enjoying a complete meal in my study, provided and prepared by someone I had never even met.

In another instance, I was thinking of new clothes. I had in mind a particular type of dress with matching jacket that was currently in fashion, but I had not the money with which to purchase it just then. Within a few days, after affirming substance as the one and only reality, a friend brought me, as a gift, the type of dress and jacket I wished, though it was far more beautiful than anything I had been able to visualize. In still another instance, when my son was in need of certain items of clothing, a friend telephoned late one night to say that she had a box of boy's clothes she wanted to give to him. She especially mentioned the items of clothing he needed as those that she had on hand in abundance, and said she would include these.

When we realize that we can gain control of substance through our attitudes, it is as though we gain control of our financial affairs, rather than feeling subject to them. As we gain this feeling of dominion, we no longer feel financially bound, limited, or discouraged; we know that we have the power to change whatever needs to be changed by changing our attitude about it. *As we begin to appreciate rather than depreciate substance, it seems to begin working very hard to please us and to meet our needs. As we think of it as the one and only reality in our lives, substance then has the power to work for us in unlimited ways for our greatest good.*

THE POWER OF SUBSTANCE

Charles Fillmore might have been summarizing the power of attitudes to mold substance when he wrote, "Substance is first given form in the mind."[3]

Never underestimate the power of substance. It underlies everything in your world and it is controlled by your ideas about it. Whether it is life, love, wisdom, power, or more financial good that you want, give substance your wholehearted attention and appreciation. It will become your obedient servant, only too happy to work with you, for you, round about you — to provide for you in every way.

A reader in New Hampshire said: "I am happy to report that shortly after I started to declare every day, 'DIVINE SUBSTANCE IS THE ONE AND ONLY REALITY IN MY LIFE AND AFFAIRS,' I obtained two new art students, got an order for the product I sell, and received the inspiration for a children's book I plan to write.

---

3. Ibid.

"As I used the affirmation, 'DIVINE SUBSTANCE APPROPRIATELY MANIFESTS FOR ME HERE AND NOW,' I had several other prosperity demonstrations. I gave my brother these statements to use, and he soon had three prosperity demonstrations in his business."

Substance is the one reality, and your understanding of this gives you the key to prosperity!

A MASTER PLAN
FOR SUCCESS

What do you want to achieve, accomplish, experience? There is a simple method that can help you attain the success you truly desire. It is the use of a master plan for success.

There is nothing new about the power of a master plan. People often use a master plan to fail. They plan for failure, and they get it. Invariably, those who succeed over a long period are those who planned for success, and got it.

As you read the biographies of great men, you find that a master plan was usually followed by them or by someone near them, interested in their success. Much of the phenomenal success of Franklin D. Roosevelt could be attributed to a master plan. Twenty years before he became President, a master plan for his success was drawn up, by a man named Louis Howe. Howe became so convinced of Roosevelt's potential as a great leader that he refused to become disturbed when Roosevelt became ill. Instead, Howe mapped out a timetable for the future success of his friend. Twenty years later, when Franklin D. Roosevelt became President, Louis Howe had the satisfaction of witnessing an achievement for which he had been planning for twenty years.

Perhaps you are thinking, "Yes, but it was easier for Roosevelt to achieve his goals, because he had wealth and influence to aid him."

The master-plan idea works, regardless of any other conditions or circumstances. If you can conceive what you wish to accomplish within the next few years, work out a timetable for your success, and then just hold to that expectation, quietly working toward it. *Your master plan will draw to you whatever else is needed to make your life as you wish it.* Such is the magnetic power of the master plan!

A DESTRUCTIVE PLAN

Adolf Hitler used the master-plan idea destructively. He was unknown in the early 1920's.

He had no money, no friends, no influence, and he was not trained for any specific work. But he did have a master plan which he outlined while in jail. In his book, *Mein Kampf,* he outlined his master plan. A recent biographer has said that World War II might have been avoided had the proper authorities taken Hitler's master plan seriously. Because he was an unknown, with only a jail record and some fantastic ideas, few believed him. But his master plan worked anyway, to the destruction of millions of people.

CHURCHILL'S SUCCESSFUL MASTER PLAN

One of the great men of recent times who had a master plan for success was Winston Churchill. Early in his career he wanted to get into public life, but he was unknown to the public. He succeeded in getting some of the English newspapers to allow him to write for them about the Cuban campaign, from India, and from various trouble spots around the world. His vivid newspaper accounts attracted a large following, and he became known to the British people. Then he began to run for various political offices. Every time he was defeated for an office, he would run for a more important one.

One biographer has said that the most mystifying aspect of the elections was Churchill's attitude when he lost: his manner was no different from that of the winner! After one defeat, Churchill turned to the winner and said, "I don't think the world has heard the last of either of us." This remark, coming from a man who had just lost an election, confused the winner so much that he rushed out to recheck the election returns, to be sure that *he* had really won. Robert Lewis Taylor has written in his biography of Churchill, "He was a master planner."

Another distinguished leader whose career indicated a knowledge of the master-plan idea was former President Charles DeGaulle of France. After World War II, he quietly retired to his country place, and it was generally assumed that his public life was over. One biographer has said that during that quiet period, lasting for twelve years, General DeGaulle spent a great deal of time in "study and meditation." He was studying his country's situation and meditating upon its return to greatness. It is little wonder that he became the one to lead France back to power.

JOSHUA'S PLAN LEADS TO
THE PROMISED LAND

There is nothing new about the master-plan idea. Some of the great men of the Bible succeeded in the face of great obstacles, through following their master plans. Perhaps one of the most outstanding examples is Joshua, one of the twelve spies Moses sent into the Promised Land. Joshua returned and described the land as rich. He brought back a great staff heavy with grapes to prove it. He stated his faith in the Hebrews' ability to go into the Promised Land immediately and possess it. But ten of the twelve spies gave negative reports, and Moses decided to wait.

The result was that the Children of Israel remained on the border of the Promised Land for forty years. During that time, Joshua served Moses in many ways. He quietly bided his time, keeping the vision of the Promised Land firmly in mind. He apparently had a detailed plan in mind for taking the land, because when he became the leader of the Hebrew people, he immediately informed them that they would pass over the Jordan into the Promised Land in just three days—and they did![1]

Fix your master plan in your mind, and keep thinking about it secretly. Then when the way begins to open for you to achieve results, you

---

1. See *The Millionaire Joshua* by Catherine Ponder, published by DeVorss & Co., 1978, Marina del Rey, California, 90291.

can do so very quickly. The longer your good is in coming, the greater it will be when it arrives!

IT PAYS TO HAVE A MASTER PLAN

A certain man was recently much in the news as a candidate for governor of his state, and a presidential candidate. During that period a stockbroker said to me: "Keep your eyes on that man. We will be hearing about him in the future, because he knows the power of the master plan."

Years before this man became president of his company, he had quietly worked out a master plan for its success. The day he became president, he took that plan out of his desk drawer and began executing it. Within a short time, his company was no longer a mediocre corporation. Its sales record during recent years has drawn national attention. This man proved that it pays to have a master plan, as he launched forth into new fields of endeavor.

A WOMAN'S DREAM PLAN COMES TRUE

I once met a woman who planned her way to success. For many years, she had nothing except hundreds of acres of pasture land, which were considered to be of little value. This land was located about a mile from the nearest highway and five miles from the nearest town. But this woman had a dream: She held in her mind the vision that one day her pasture land would become one of the most beautiful suburban shopping centers in the country.

In a few years, the nearby military base was enlarged. A four-lane highway was built, and it bordered on this woman's pasture land. Immediately realtors began making offers to purchase the land. But she did not want to sell it — she wanted to develop it. She refused all offers and held on to her dream, though for financial reasons it would have seemed wise to sell.

Months went by, and then one day she noticed a contractor with his men and equipment working on property adjoining hers. She explained her dream to the contractor; he assured her that her dream could materialize, and that he would help. He suggested formation of a corporation in which she would furnish the land, and he would furnish equipment and men, and do the contracting and building. He explained that he had a wealthy friend who would provide financial backing and become the necessary third party in the corporation.

Today, the woman is president of that corporation, which owns a housing development, an apartment development, and a colonial-style shopping center—one of the most beautiful in the country. She had a plan, a vision. She dared to hold to her plan, and now she has all that she dared to envision, and more!

DON'T COMPROMISE YOUR PLAN

When you gain the vision of your master plan, refuse all offers of compromise or halfway success; quietly wait for the right situation to present itself before putting your plan into action. If you compromise once, you will have to keep on compromising, and the result will not be one of satisfying success.

Also, keep quiet about your master plan. Don't try to get somebody else's approval of it. Don't try to convince anyone else that you are right. The doubts of others can dissipate your dream. If you keep quiet about your dreams and keep believing in them, the same Power that gave you those dreams will give you the opportunities and all that is necessary for making them come true—at the right time, under the right circumstances.

A businessman had been in financial difficulties for some time. He heard about the master-plan idea, and he devised a master plan for his business that covered a five-year period. For months and months, he worked on this master plan, but nothing happened. Finally, through conversation with a friend who had introduced him to the master-plan idea, he realized why his plan was not working: He was trying to convince his wife and his mother-in-law that at last he was going to become a success. They kept doubting this, and their critical attitudes were neutralizing everything he was trying to do.

He saw that it was not necessary for him to convince them of his planned success. Instead, as he quietly invoked his master plan, saying nothing, the successful results did their own convincing.

A friend who has become financially independent through his stock-market transactions in recent years states that one of the reasons for his success is that he never discusses his business affairs with anyone. He affirms guidance in his financial affairs, quietly follows whatever leads come, and says nothing. Early in the course of his transactions, he lost $20,000. If he had mentioned it to his family, they would have urged him not to invest anything more — and they would have missed out on the fortune that he has since made on the stock market. "In quietness and in confidence shall be your strength." (Isaiah 30:15)

A Pulitzer prize winner once gave this worthwhile advice: "When you have laid out a course of action for yourself, calculate the risks ahead

and then go through with your course of action,
no matter what is going on. Don't be flurried
and don't get panicky. The man who stops to
take counsel of his fears is the man who is lost.
Safety and success lie ahead and nowhere else.
No one ever reaches them if he stops to worry
about the unseen."

IMPOSSIBLE DREAM COMES TRUE

A lawyer began invoking the master-plan idea
early in his career. He and his father shared two
small law offices with their secretaries. These
offices were located in an old building on the
town square, amid much noise. One day the son
dictated to his secretary a master plan for the
firm's growth during the next five years.

He stated in detail his desires for the firm. He
wanted to expand from a two-man law firm to a
five-man or six-man firm, which would include
a trial lawyer, a tax specialist, and a junior
member to handle much of the detail work. He
wanted each lawyer to have his own secretary,
with a principal secretary who would be in
charge of the others. He desired new, comfort-
able, air-conditioned offices. He set down the
increase in income he desired for the firm, year
by year, over the five-year period. At the time

he dictated all these expectations, it seemed an impossible dream. In the following months he often reviewed his master plan.

Soon a third man, talented as a trial lawyer, came into the firm. A whole floor of new offices was offered the firm in a bank building. These new offices included a conference room and a kitchen, in addition to ample space for each attorney and secretary. A fourth lawyer who had just finished law school was employed. He became the junior member and relieved the other lawyers of many detailed assignments. The income of the firm mounted. Later, a tax specialist joined the firm. Today that law firm is one of the most prominent in the state. The man who devised and invoked the master plan for its success recently served as president of an international service organization. Such is the power of the master plan: not only does it work in ways we can foresee and plan for, it also provides us with blessings beyond what we can envision.

MAKE YOUR MASTER PLAN DEFINITE

Success comes when you move unerringly forward, rejecting all that tends to distract you from your master plan. You are well equipped to live life fully and to master life in its every

phase, if you dare to work out a master plan of
your desires (in as much detail as possible) for
the next few years and then dwell quietly upon it. It is good to list dates by which you wish
certain desires fulfilled. (But then dare to be
flexible.)

When we become definite and positive in our
thinking, even as regards the time element, it is
as though we tap a special power in the universe
which rushes forth to arrange events, causing
our stipulated results to appear by the specified
dates. Often we let our desired good slip by us
because we do not list our desires and the dates
by which we wish them to appear as visible, satisfying results in our lives.

I once met a young man who was already on
the way to becoming a millionaire. He stated
that his success began at the age of eighteen,
when he dared to work out a twelve-year plan
for his success. He wanted to be financially independent at the age of thirty. After working
out his master plan, it not only began to work,
but gained momentum, so that his desires had
been completely fulfilled several years before his
thirtieth birthday.

*Never underestimate the power of the master
plan. It is scientific, it is practical, it is business-
like, and it works!* Even though your master
plan may not produce immediate results, if you

will develop it and keep thinking about it, you will feed it with your mind power and with your faith. Eventually all obstacles will be dissolved and you will enter your "promised land."

BE PREPARED TO ACCEPT YOUR ABUNDANCE

Here is a final point to remember: Success has a way of coming in a hurry after you have endured a "long haul" of plodding along slowly. As you quietly persist toward your goal, prepare yourself for quick, exciting, success-filled results. Have your plans made as to what you will do when success arrives, because just when it may seem least likely, the tide can turn for you. Then it will be necessary for you to take a deep breath, and proceed to accept your abundance of good.

As fulfillment comes, you must not let it unbalance you. Be alert and ready to accept it; otherwise, it may slip away, leaving you to begin all over again. If you have a master plan, it will be easier for you to accept your success and maintain it.

To paraphrase the words of Paul: "Forget the things that are behind. Press forward toward your goal!" Now, as you work out your master plan for success, affirm: "DIVINE INTELLIGENCE,

LET THE MASTER PLAN OF MY LIFE NOW REVEAL IT-
SELF TO ME. LET THE MASTER PLAN OF MY LIFE
NOW BEGIN WORKING FOR ME. I GIVE THANKS FOR
MY MASTER PLAN OF SUCCESS. I GIVE THANKS FOR
THE PERFECT RESULTS OF THAT MASTER PLAN.
WITH GOD'S HELP I NOW PLAN MY WAY TO SUC-
CESS; WITH GOD'S HELP I NOW BEGIN TO EXPERI-
ENCE THE RESULTS OF MY MASTER PLAN."

TITHE YOUR WAY
TO PROSPERITY

— Chapter 4 —

Charles Fillmore has written, "Tithing is based upon a law that cannot fail, and it is the surest way ever found to demonstrate plenty, for it is God's own law and way of giving."[1] The truth of this has been proved again and again. I once knew two professional men who were partners. One tithed; the other did not. The one who did not tithe made around twenty thousand dollars a year. He worked nights, days, and weekends, and still could not "get by" financially. There were frequent spells of illness and unexpected mishaps in his family. The

1. Fillmore, *Prosperity*

harder he worked, the more he had to work. Collecting money owed him was difficult.

His business associate made about twelve thousand dollars a year, and he tithed. He seemed to live much better; his family seemed to have more. Surely they enjoyed life more. This man never thought of working nights or weekends; his clients liked him and paid their accounts without protest or delay. Finally, after several years, he left the partnership and went out on his own. Soon he was making a great deal more money than his former partner made. He put God first financially, and the Lord prospered him.

GOD AS YOUR FINANCIAL PARTNER MAKES THE DIFFERENCE

Charles Fillmore has further written:[2]

By the act of tithing, men make God their partner in their financial transactions and thus keep the channel open from the source in the ideal to the manifestation in the realm of things. Whoever thinks that he is helping to keep God's work going in the earth cannot help but believe that God will help him. This virtually makes God not only a silent partner but

---

2. *Ibid.*

also active in producing capital from unseen and unknown sources, in opening up avenues for commercial gain, and in various other ways making the individual prosperous.

A woman once told me that she and another member of her family held identical shares of stock. During a time of financial stress, she decided to sell her stock; she made only a few hundred dollars' profit from the sale. The other member of the family, who tithed faithfully from all channels of income, prayed for guidance and decided to hold his stock a little longer. A few weeks later he sold it for a profit of $6,000! This woman realized that if she, too, had had faith in the tithing law of prosperity, expecting it to prosper and protect her, guidance would have come, meeting her financial need in some other way, so that she also would have made a $6,000 profit, instead of only a few hundred dollars. Needless to say, she is now a consistent tither of all her income.

THE BEST INVESTMENT YOU CAN MAKE

L. E. Meyer says in *As You Tithe So You Prosper*[3] that we make things at least ten times

3. *Published for free distribution by Unity School of Christianity, Unity Village, Missouri 64065.*

easier when we honor the Lord with our tithe; that in tithing we substitute faith in God's supply for fear that we shall come to want; and that tithing is a law of financial liberty. He has written: "The story of tithing both ancient and modern declares it to be the best investment we can make. It does more good than the most generous giving that is done only on the impulse of the moment." And we can see why: Just as it is necessary to breathe out regularly in order to receive fresh air into the lungs, so it is necessary to give regularly if we wish to receive regularly. From a business standpoint, we prefer a definite, systematic, regular income to an occasional, undetermined inflow of money, which may or may not be financially sufficient. "Whatsoever a man soweth, that shall he also reap." If we do not sow, we do not reap.

In loosing the purse strings we loose many other things that have bound us, so that we are free from the unhappy, unnecessary, unwanted experiences of life. I know from my own experience how much healthier I have been since I began tithing several decades ago. Whenever I hear of loss, theft, accident, illness, and the high emotional and financial costs that usually accompany these experiences, I cannot help thinking: "It's too bad those persons do not tithe. They would doubtless be protected from such negative and unhappy experiences."

JACOB'S SUCCESS COVENANT

Truly the Bible gives us the promise of prosperity and protection when we tithe. The first instance of tithing is found in the life of Abram, who tithed a "tenth of all" to the priest, Melchizedek (and the tenth must have been a considerable amount, because Abram was described as "very rich in cattle, in silver, and in gold" [Genesis 13:2]).

Abram apparently passed along his belief in the prosperity law of tithing, because his grandson Jacob knew of its power. After Jacob left his father's house and went forth to seek his fortune in a new land, he made a prosperity covenant with the Lord: "If God will be with me, and will keep me in this way that I go, and will give me bread to eat, and raiment to put on, so that I come again to my father's house in peace, and Jehovah will be my God, . . . of all that thou shalt give me I will surely give the tenth unto thee." (Genesis 28:20-22)

In this passage Jacob clearly indicated that he expected his practice of tithing to protect and prosper him, as well as to reestablish harmony between himself and his family. The Bible reveals that all these blessings and more came to Jacob: "And the man increased exceedingly, and had large flocks, and maid-servants and men-servants, and camels and asses." (Genesis

30:43). When he later decided to return to the
land of his birth and to attempt reconciliation
with his brother Esau, whose birthright he had
earlier stolen, he sent ahead rich gifts to Esau.
When he and his brother were reconciled, Esau
tried to return the gifts to Jacob; but Jacob said,
"Take, I pray thee, my gift that is brought to
thee; because God hath dealt graciously with
me." (Genesis 33:11)[4]

TEN—THE MYSTICAL NUMBER OF INCREASE

Throughout the Bible the tithe is mentioned
as a "tenth of all," because ten was considered
by the ancients to be a mystical number symbol-
izing increase. Solomon, whose great wealth is
familiar to us, emphasized the prospering power
of giving first of one's income, rather than
waiting until other needs have been met, when
he said: "Honor Jehovah with thy substance,
And with the first-fruits of all thine increase: So
shall thy barns be filled with plenty, And thy

---

4. See Chapter 5, *The Millionaires of Genesis* (1976)
published by DeVorss & Co., Marina del Rey, California,
90291.

vats shall overflow with new wine." (Proverbs 3:9,10)

As long as the Hebrews tithed and honored the Lord with a tenth of all their income, they were prospered. However, it was pointed out during the Restoration Period by the prophet Malachi, that because they were no longer tithing they had fallen into hard times. During this period, corruption was prevalent in every form: the Hebrews were intermarrying with other groups who did not worship Jehovah; there was a high divorce rate; deceit, robbery, and all types of violence prevailed. Malachi pointed out that better times would again come if the people would again put God first financially: "Bring ye the whole tithe into the storehouse, . . . and prove me now herewith, saith Jehovah of hosts, if I will not open you the windows of heaven, and pour you out a blessing, that there shall not be room enough *to receive it*." (Malachi 3:10) Malachi promised not only renewed blessings of prosperity but renewed protection for their crops: "And I will rebuke the devourer for your sakes, and he shall not destroy the fruits of your ground; neither shall your vine cast its fruit before the time in the field. . . . And all nations shall call you happy; for ye shall be a delightsome land, saith Jehovah of hosts." (Malachi 3:11,12)

JESUS AND TITHING

Sometimes people say, "Well, I'm not under the Old Testament laws, because I'm a Christian, and I follow only the Jesus Christ teachings." Of course as Christians we believe in and apply the spiritual teachings of the entire Bible. However, Jesus Christ also set forth the prosperity law of tithing. During New Testament times the temple (as well as the later work of the early Christians) was supported by tithes. Jesus clearly indicated His belief in tithing in parable; and once, when addressing a group of Pharisees, He made it plain that His followers should establish the right attitude toward tithing: "Ye tithe mint and anise and cummin, and have left undone the weightier matters of the law, justice, and mercy, and faith: but these ye ought to have done, and not to have left the other undone." (Matthew 23:23)

Paul pointed out that if the early Christians gave consistently, it would not be necessary to take offerings for his journeys: "Upon the first day of the week let each one of you lay by him in store, as he may prosper, that no collections be made when I come." (I Corinthians 16:2)

The prosperity of any individual, nation, or organization that tithes rests on a firm founda-

tion. Jesus might have been summarizing the power of the prosperity law of tithing when He advised: "Give, and it shall be given unto you; good measure, pressed down, shaken together, running over, shall they give into your bosom. For with what measure ye mete it shall be measured to you again." (Luke 6:38)

NOW IS THE TIME TO TITHE

Whatever your financial condition of the moment—even if, like the Children of Israel, you are in a financial wilderness or a state of financial dissatisfaction—you can be prosperous. You need not wait until "things get better" or until you "get out of debt" to begin living under the prosperity law of tithing. Right now, you should begin bringing divine order into your affairs by honoring God with a "tenth of all" income, as soon as you receive it. You can be assured that, like the Children of Israel, you will be led into the Promised Land of greater prosperity.

A reader from Ohio reported:

It is a mystery to me how it is possible for me to tithe ten percent gross of all the money I receive when I am on welfare. Yet since I have done this faithfully, I have had everything I needed! As I continue to put God first financially, I expect to be guided to satisfactory work so that I no longer have to depend upon welfare payments.

A businessman from New York wrote:

I started a savings account ten years ago. On paydays I would put money in. Within two weeks I would find myself having to take it out. Since I have been tithing, I haven't had to touch my savings account, except to put in more money. I am now able to pay my bills, buy food for my family, and still have enough left over for other expenses. Thanks to tithing, I expect this to be our best year ever!

THE MANY BENEFITS OF TITHING

If you are already prosperous and successful, you can be assured that you shall remain so as long as you put God first financially. If the time ever comes when you feel that your tithe is "too much" or that you can no longer afford to give so much, simply put such thoughts out of your mind. If you stop tithing, you may find yourself back in a financial wilderness, with your income greatly diminished. This can be avoided by continuing to give a "tenth of all," regardless of the amount. Indeed, if your tithe becomes large, praise and give thanks that you have so much to give. *He who practices tithing will have more to give than he thought possible before.*

A reader from Michigan wrote:

My success covenant tithe includes a tithe from my last Social Security check. I have never saved money this way in my whole life. Neither have I given a like amount to any church, nor have I ever tithed before. *What amazes me is how easily the money accumulates, and that I don't even miss what I give away.* Furthermore, I find myself giving gladly and gratefully. My life is really changing since I have begun this prayer-and-giving method. The skin condition I suffered from for five years is now healed, and I feel happier and more fulfilled than at any time in my long life.

A Californian reported:

I made my first tithing success covenant the first of last year. I started with a goal a little higher than I would normally achieve. After one week of fantastic business, I increased the amount I wanted to receive for the month of January, promising in my covenant to tithe ten percent of everything I received to God's work, or to whomever or wherever I gained the spiritual insight and help I was trying to attain. Then I really worked to keep the old negative patterns of lack and limitation out of my mind.

The results? *I made almost as much money in the month of January as I had made during the entire previous year!* But even more important than that, I am learning how to have a prosperity consciousness rather than a pattern of lack and limitation. What a difference that makes.

One of the greatest fears of many wealthy people is the fear of losing their money. I once knew a millionaire in the construction business who literally worried himself into ill health, according to his doctors, though to all appearances he had nothing to worry about. It took me only a few minutes in conversing with him to discover that his greatest concern was about losing his money. Since the prosperity law of tithing promises protection in every way, no such fear need assail those who tithe.

MAKE YOUR OWN SUCCESS COVENANT

No matter where you are on the ladder of success, why not follow the example of Jacob, who made a definite prosperity covenant with the Lord? You might even paraphrase his words in writing out your own covenant or agreement with the Lord: "Knowing that God will be with me, and will help me attain the success and prosperity that I know are mine by divine right—the perfect supply of food, clothing, housing, and property that are divinely mine—so that my life may be fruitful and satisfying, and so that harmony, peace, good health, and prosperity shall reign supreme. . . for all these blessings and for all other blessings with which I am and shall be divinely endowed, I will begin immediately to give a tenth of all my income to God's work. I will gladly honor the Lord with my substance and with the first fruits of all my increase."

If you wish to simplify your prosperity agreement, you may write out and affirm often the last statement of Jacob's covenant: "Of all that thou shalt give me, I will surely give the tenth unto thee." (Genesis 28:22) Or you can use the words of Solomon: "I will honor the Lord with my substance and with the first fruits of all my increase." (Proverbs 3:9)[5]

Try making your covenant for a definite period—a month, six months, or a year. As a part of the agreement, you may want to list any definite results you wish to attain during that period, showing a definite future date by which you

---

5. If you wish to obtain a free copy of the author's Success Covenant, write her requesting it.

wish those results to unfold. Then place your written covenant in a safe place where no one will see or disturb it. Begin tithing immediately and regularly of the first fruits of all your increase, even before paying bills or meeting needs of any kind. At regular intervals, perhaps once a month, check your written covenant to see what listed results have been obtained, marking them off your list and giving thanks. At the conclusion of your first covenant period, you will be ready to venture forth and make another covenant with the Lord, concerning your prosperity plans, hopes, and desires for another stipulated period, and continue tithing, giving thanks to God for each result.[6]

A businessman from Ohio said:

I prepare a new success covenant for myself every four to five months, and it is such a thrill to realize how many of the items listed have been achieved. I enjoy using the suggested words of Truth which help keep me on the right track. Also, it is a pleasure to share my good fortune through my tithes. Such systematic and generous giving makes me feel rich.

As you begin using this prosperity method of tithing and making a covenant with God con-

6. See chapter on "The Prospering Power of a Success Covenant" in *The Millionaires of Genesis.*

cerning your financial affairs, you will probably become so fascinated with its power for progress and achievement that you will want to increase your tithe another ten percent. Joel Goldsmith has written: "Interestingly enough, rarely does tithing stop at ten percent. I have known three different people who tithed eighty percent of all their income and, surprising as it may seem, these people had more left to live on, and with, than they could possibly spend even if they were very extravagant."

A SPECIAL NOTE FROM THE AUTHOR

Through the generous outpouring of their tithes over the years, the readers of my books have helped me to financially establish three new churches—the most recent being a global ministry, the nondenominational *Unity Church Worldwide,* with headquarters in Palm Desert, California. Many thanks for your help in the past, and for all that you continue to share.

You are also invited to share your tithes with the churches of your choice—especially those which teach the truths stressed in this book. Such churches would include the metaphysical churches of Unity, Religious Science, Divine

Science, Science of Mind and other related churches, many of which are members of the International New Thought Movement. (For a list of such churches write The International New Thought Alliance, 7314 E. Stetson Drive, Scottsdale, Arizona 85251.) Your support of such churches can help spread the prosperous Truth that mankind is now seeking in this New Age of metaphysical enlightenment.